$\mathcal{P}$IANO in the $\mathcal{V}$INEYARD

For Rosanna,
   with hope that you can
hear the music.

Jean Janzen
Nov. 8, 2004

Piano in the Vineyard

poems by
award-winning poet

Jean Janzen

Good Books

Intercourse, PA 17534

800/762-7171 • www.goodbks.com

Acknowledgments

Grateful acknowledgment is made to the editors of the following publications
where these poems first appeared:
*Christian Century, Christianity & Literature, The Common Reader,
Great River Review, The Mennonite, Poetry International,* and *Ruah.*
"Wilderness" was chosen for the anthology *First Fruits.*

Cover photography by Louis Janzen
Design by Dawn J. Ranck

PIANO IN THE VINEYARD
First published in 2004 by Good Books, Intercourse, PA 17534
Copyright © 2004 by Jean Janzen
International Standard Book Number: 1-56148-429-6
Library of Congress Catalog Card Number: 2004001235

Library of Congress Cataloging-in-Publication Data

Janzen, Jean.
  Piano in the vineyard / by Jean Janzen.
     p. cm.
  ISBN 1-56148-429-6
  I. Title.
PS3560.A5364P53 2004
811'.54--dc22   2004001235

For Louis

and in memory of Roberta Spear, 1948-2003

Table of Contents

Broken Places

Egrets

When the creek sinks
into quiet pools
and the sky hardens
into winter-gray slate,
they come back
one at a time,
the white egret,
simple in her full
attention, like
a lily.
But today
I am astonished
at their number—
ten, a flock.
With slow crank of wings
they fly in and out
of the green pines
and cluster around
a muddy pool,
what remains
from the dam's
last spill.
I want them
to be alone
and statuary
as before, not
this agitation,
their necks bobbing,

brown muck splashing
against their white
breasts. As though
isolation had been
pretense all along,
and they bend now
toward earth
and each other,
up to their knees
in commotion.

In January

January with its thumping
in the walls, gray stairs
of fog that go nowhere,
like the Winchester house—
the wife of the gunmaker
haunted by the dead.
Day and night, carpenters
hammering to keep out
the ghosts.

*

I think of Richie, my first
love, whose gun went off
into his heart as he
oiled the barrel. Thirteen,
the Kansas sky like sheet metal,
wind in a howl.

*

January's dip into vengeance.
After the Birth, the hunting.
Herod still alive, and Jesus
in Egypt. His mother clutching
him against desert storm,
her robe flying.

*

May the Lord's wrath be triggered.
May he break their teeth,
may he seat them at long tables
in unheated, windowless factories.
May they disassemble each gun
through my sleepless nights.
For the Child returns, his small
hands scattering the proud
like winter birds, laughing.

Another World

It happens again, the stare,
as if another world calls to her,
her slow fall, and our clatter of keys stops—

my high school typing teacher lying
sprawled on the floor, white hair
in disarray, her arms caught in stiff gesture.

And we stare, silent,
our black sentences strung out
before us until she comes back,

her face softening as she rises,
smooths her hair and woolen skirt.
Then, once again, this room, the clock,

typewriter bells warning us
to swing the carriages back, to keep
our words within margins,

here where we glimpsed what we feared,
that our bodies are not really ours,
that something could claim us

and carry us into another place.
Was it death or terror I saw
in Miss Finn's face? And what was it

that she saw in mine when she
stood again and looked into my eyes,
when she asked, "Where were we?"

April Storm

"You have noted my lamentation:
put my tears into your bottle." Psalm 56

These widening days can't hold
our grief, the entire landscape
too narrow. Hail on the green
blaze of grass. Thick sky breaks
over the cherry trees. Thundersnow.
Red lace of the Japanese maple
whipped and torn, bruised faces
of pansies swaying on thin necks.
No rescue except for the tears.
Cold glass against the cheek
and pulled away, our collected ache
bending the shelf of the universe.

I think of Chopin, the pages
sliding off the piano keys in Majorca,
his coughing as he inks the notes,
door flung open to a wild sky.
Each note a shoring up against loss,
like this plum tree—under the drift
of petals, its roots clutching
the earth like claws. And those
marble lions perched at the edge
of the sea who gaze at the relentless
churning. This is our story,
the various pitches of its telling.
In the gray dawn, one lion rises
to lift his aria in a roar.
The wet pink of his tongue.

After Reading Genesis Again

So much weeping at the end, their shoulders
shaking, men thrown upon each other's
necks in recognition and regret. Brothers
in one room. I love the story, the father
sending his famished, guilty sons for food
to the dreamer Joseph, who stands before
them in silken robes, their futures bare.
How he leaves them to wail in his own room.

Sometimes at night I think I hear men's groans
piled up for centuries. Sobs and repentance,
some wasted, and some never done. Slow dance
of hatred unresolved, the bitter bone.
And women. Rachel and Leah feuding still;
clawing of branches on my windowsill.

Two Rocks

Two small rocks in my desk,
one for each hand—

the one from Jerusalem
worn to a glaze,

the other a piece of dull
brick from the foundation

of my birthplace.
Two for the journey,

dumb and still until
I rattle the drawer

reaching for my pen.
One from the glacier-scraped

north, the other from the old
seabed lifted into Mount Zion.

One for the dismantled house
and the wheat swaying over it,

there where I first cried out,
where the aurora borealis played,

and my mother's face grew pale
as the baby stopped breathing.

And the other for the Man
who walked on that mountain,

who had no home,
for his broad, open hands,

and for his weeping.

Eating Popcorn

I was standing on the place
in Hiroshima where the bomb
fell, reciting a poem
fifty years after,

that memorial of burned shadows,
a single metal skeleton,
and ropes of folded cranes.
We prayed for peace

under plum trees and over
the layers of samurai blades,
torn flags, the piled skulls.
Here earth exploded

out of the sea. Now mountains
turn their faces in shame
because words are fickle
and disappear, because my neighbor's

family is ash, because we said
"oh look," college kids in 1953.
Driving through New Mexico
when the test-cloud rose

in our sight, we ate popcorn
and laughed, flirted,
and fell asleep.

Tuning the Piano

He tunes, but seldom plays,
asking me to test his work

with Chopin or a bit of jazz
when he is done. His ear

still true for pitch as we
swap stories. This time Japan

from which I have just returned.
Three days after Nagasaki's bombing

he was sent in to search
through the rubble for prisoners

of war. His arms are knobby
with radiation scars, the only one

from his platoon still alive.
He remembers the Japanese schoolchildren

who, seeing the soldiers approach,
assumed they would be killed.

The teacher commanded them to sing—
"Sing into the face of death!"

And so they sang, terrified, until
the soldiers laid down their guns.

Fifty years later he can play
the tune still, and he does.

New Spaces

God's will is the whole backyard,
someone said. Sleep in the hammock,
or sweat with the spade—
it's roomy and permissive.
But what we find, digging or dreaming,
is too huge to be contained,
tree roots thrusting into the next yard,
the sky dropping its thunder
into the whole neighborhood.
                    This cancer
in your body, wild and voracious,
moves mountains higher than our faith.
God's will is large as the universe,
the treatments hurling against
our spinning earth, and we tilt
in ache and prayers. The horizon
no longer familiar, we are bumped
into new spaces where we float,
separate and together, in the dark.

Squirrel Hanging

The dead body is draped over
the electric wire which killed him.

It hangs in clear view where I walk
below its slow decay. A decade,

it seems, of resistance
to this valley's fire and fog.

After the crumble of skin,
the small triangle of skull,

symmetry of ribs, limp legs swinging
in the wind, and finally

only the spine still clinging.
And I am reminded of the martyr cages

in Münster still hanging
on the church tower, where birds

once exposed the delicate metatarsals
of feet wildly dancing for New Jerusalem.

Empty cages, the bars like skeletons
which resist the loss of memory

that once someone dared to walk
the wire out in the open, the sun

blinding his eyes so that he failed
to see the broken place,

where he stepped, and where he died,
exposed and forgiven.

Giving Up Vengeance

Sometimes we think we know how
to give it up, when the sun once again
grazes our backs after cold wind.

But even then, those patches of ice
glare from shadowed corners;
spring comes reluctantly.

I watch the children who forgive
easily—beatings, the biting words.
But then, memory, buried glacial hate.

How shall we sing *"Ich Grolle Nicht"* *
after the broken heart, like Jack did
in that dusty high school room?

Fifteen, blonde curls and round face,
he sings Schumann's forgiveness
as I press the piano keys, notes stacked

into chords to make a space
for the pain which rises and falls,
promising no rancor. The sweet tenor

voice, precise pronunciation,
that song, which presses itself now
against my own angers. Jack and I

walking out together into the clean wind,
the frozen plowed fields around us,
row after black row lifted by the blade.

* *"I hold no resentment"*

Wailing in the Shower

After the elation of giving birth,
our new daughter fed and sleeping,
I stand under the warm water
and begin on the high notes—
Madame Butterfly's ecstasy,
One fine day in May, the harmony
sliding over my body.

*

After the loss of his bride,
our friend turns on the guestroom
shower and begins his long wailing.
It echoes throughout the house,
flows down the stairway,
his baritone cries rising and falling.
Over and over, the full octaves.

*

This narrow passage
from birth to death,
like lines of song on a page,
our first wail carrying us
on breath and air toward
the final water.
Butterfly bows as far
as she can. Her son
is that small figure waving,
and behind him the shining bay
blinds our eyes.

Broken Places

We know that the mountains
can't heal us, even as they stand
beside us, serene after their own
great upheaval. And from the deep,

the hidden springs rise.
"For my irregular heart," my father
said, soaking in the sulphurous pool,
the rain sizzling around him.

On the other side of the world
Mitsuko and I strip and scrub,
then enter the tranquil heat.
Like sisters, no need to speak,

for the water has claimed us,
holding us above the rush
of the river. All of us shipwrecked,
clutching what we can,

no cure except the final one.
But here, for awhile, our bodies release
the secret aches. Holding nothing
but water in our arms, we lean

against the split and tumbled sides
of rocks, here where the mountain's heart
spills out, holding us in its own
broken place, the mists rising.

The Garden

Naming It: A Garden Cycle

January

New Year's Day ritual, my husband
begins to prune his roses.
Soul-work, he calls it, cuts
new spaces into the gray air.
As when I turned twelve
and cut off my braids, stored them
in an empty chocolate box.

Dead Peace roses into the trash can,
Double Delights, the John F. Kennedys.
Under January's milky eye,
little racks of stems, cut ends scabbing.

It is done. I see myself
in the mirror, hair loose around
my face. Hair dresser has turned
her back, gathering scissors and comb.
Somewhere behind her a door
opens to a raw wind.

February

Fig tree dominates the garden,
gray and knobby against gray fog,
its bare branches grotesque.
Like the old, bent parishioners
my father would visit, taking me
along, a child. They stroked
my hands, my woolen dress,
reached out with cloudy eyes.

This tree reaches everywhere,
as though light can be caught.
Slow sun drains through, stirs
a wing. Then one morning
I see them, green tips of figs
hard as emeralds escaping
from every knuckled grasp.

March

Mother on the northern prairie,
weary of white and the smell of wet wool,
the children quarreling. Thirty-one days
until April and its first crocus.
She sits by the afternoon window,
sun ripening like the child
within her, and pierces a pillowcase
with yellow daisies, needle flashing through.

Here the crows have begun their complaining
again. Daffodils already snuffed
and turning to paper, iris unfolding
its standards and falls, tulips,
anemones, their black centers. And the crows
skim across the garden tying it together—
icy wind and blade, the woman at the window.

April

April now with its explosions
of plum and lamb, such loose
tenderness in the wind.
The trees undo their knots,
reckless, the sap resolute.
The month Grandmother turned
her back and entered the barn
to end her life among the animals.
She kicks the stool away and writhes,
the animals chewing, listening.

Do we love the blossom
for its fragility or the way
its center clings? If only
Grandmother had touched the calf,
stroked its ears, sat down
beside it and listened to its breathing,
their rib cages lifting and falling together.

May

Hollow pit of the sky deepens
its arch, and the farmer plows
his field. Dry earth, dry petals,
as life is parceled out,
some fields fallow, some green,
canals diverting their silver.

May, the month of burials,
cancer's victory. In a dream
my brother, father of five, returns
to me with a strong embrace
and the cure. Coconut milk, he says,
as if heaven is in Hawaii, as if
he wants me to stay, to love this life first.

June

Now the sun early and late
on our heads. Holiness
come close, singeing our hair.
Work for the night is coming,
our fathers sang. The pickers
sweat in the orchards,
truckers drag their huge loads.

I think of the chef in the movie
who chooses to stay with his recipes
and kitchen pots, waves goodbye
to his red-haired love,
how she bakes his cakes until she dies.
Long light, all of us burning.

July

Power surge, everything under
the blue canopy swelling with heat.
Pressure into sugar, cotton bolls
stretching. And body-swell.
We touch carefully or not at all.
Hot wires falling in storms.
Sisters clasping hands to run
away from the lightning
as it flares through them both.

Sometimes it's words. A woman listening
to my poem, the one about her, a war orphan
in my gym class doing jumping jacks.
All these years and no touching.
Something waiting to break loose.

August

Bumblebees in their awkward flight
dive into clusters of naked lady lilies.
Black against pale pink again and again.

Satiation as heat hammers away,
the grass turning pale. Air thick as plastic,
ripe to the verge of rot and split,

knife in a sweaty hand. The naked ladies
thrive, heavy with themselves, Rubens bends
toward the canvas, steps back.

Weight of flesh lifting into cloudy pinks,
buttocks unashamed. The smell of earth's tilt,
time's ooze. We sip and we swallow,

seal each day like a jar for the cellar.
More than enough.

September

After summer's overflow,
the calm, the need to hold it

carefully. The garden begins
its ruin, still holding its light.

Like the ceremonial cup
that is turned three times,

then the bow, the sip.
What are the words for communion?

No one spoke, writes Ryoto,
guest, host, the white chrysanthemum.

October

Sky like lapis lazuli,
a dome, opaque and polished.
I walk under its weight,
a sorrow that has no name.
How to find it, to speak it
with the breath spaced correctly,
tones in deepest color?
To intone as in Noh drama,
the narrator studying for years
to plant the vowels deep
in the abdomen, his muscles
becoming stone. How to hear it?
The prophet sets out
a basket of harvest fruit:
Woe to them that are at ease.
Sun dips into its dusty bed.
Time for the sifting, for the chaff
to lift, to find the essential vowel,
name on the tip of the tongue.

November

The last duck has been taken
by the fox, its skeleton on the hill,
clean as the moon, first rain
washing it. Figs sweet
and dark as coal, the arithmetic
of plus and plus before the turning.
On last warm evenings the vixen,
sleek and weary, saunters
into the garden and begins
her barking lament, and my husband,
kneeling in weeds, answers.

December

Now fog gathers to muffle
all distinctions, consonants lost.
Deodar cedars bend their tips
under the weight of crows.
And finally a flock of waxwings
flutters among the thorns
of the pyracantha, stripping
it in a frenzy.

It is time. I stand at the table
and ladle flaming cherries over
frozen cream—*righteousness
and peace kissing*, the Psalmist sings.
And the garden watches, wordless,
tapping the window glass
with its wooden hands.

This Reckless Journey

for my newborn

You began in a swirling mist
before any garden, you,
my tiny one, my insistent.

Before I was green and opening,
you were already pulsing
toward me on the far road,

small, wise traveler who
has ridden the steep tunnels
of thousands before me,

pushing through barriers
and taking light from anyone.
And I thought you were only mine.

Holding you, I remember
how I, a child, pressed against
tomato leaves in a night game

of hide-and-seek and inhaled
a pungency that was large and far,
something that could take me in

then, and now as I wash you,
your slippery body arching
toward mine, a shifting shelter,

both of us on this reckless journey.

Dandelion

I wanted to give you
a piece of paradise
to hold in your hand,
a globe of order
so that your heart
wouldn't break.

And what I found
trembled on one
pale green tube,
glistened in its precise
silks, each hot seed
still clinging.

And you ran, clumsy toddler,
and fell with it.
And the breath of your wailing
became the new order,
which, after all,
was what I had given you,
and which you couldn't hold.

Wisteria

The wisteria in its gnarled
    aging tries on the youthful
        silks again. It smothers

the arbor with heavy bloom,
    then climbs the crowns of maples,
        hangs purple pendants everywhere.

Old mother-map of the earth,
    its seductions of mud and light,
        the twisted need to bind.

Not until the shatterings
    of autumn when the tangled
        skeleton lies exposed

do I see the contortions
    of my loving, and how
        you stand alone.

Marigold

For twenty years Mary has looked
at me, Vladimir's icon over

the kitchen sink, there on the windowsill
beside the pot of Chinese jade

and the jar of marigolds. Her cheek
presses against the cheek of the Child;

her eyes are black as coal.
Window behind her, the garden

watching her watch me while
I wash the skillet and the knives,

while I sing along with Madame Butterfly,
the part where she and Suzuki

fill the room with blossoms.
And Mary's eyes smolder,

for she will never give him up.
And she is looking at me.

Hollyhock

Those summer days we pinched off
the bloom to make ballerinas,
bud for the head, sticky stamen

under the silky skirts, and then
the whirling. Beauty and desire
in their bright confusions.

In Sunday school we didn't sing
about Rahab or Bathsheba, but later
found them in Matthew's genealogy,

girls in secret, our fingers tracing
the lineage. That long red rope
reaching into the trembling Mary,

those strands of love and terror
that spread inside her like fire.
We couldn't speak their names.

But today I will sing them all.
And I will dance every syllable
of Zerubbabel, Hezekiah, and Uriah,

the long vowels of Boaz,
and the frantic twirls of Tamar.
A new testament song and dance—

mud flying, ribbons swirling
among the weeping and the laughter,
my heels and toes marking

the consonants, my voice
cracking on the high notes
where the light comes in.

Eve's Hair

after the painting by Lukas Cranach

Her body is a pale curve,
    her face an open flower.

Almost life-size, she stands
    held in a frame

against the velvet dark,
    her long, yellow locks

spiraling around her.
    She is not contained.

Adam will step across
    the border and become lost

in her flying silk,
    their union a wild glory

which they will carry
    into the rocky landscape.

Among thorns and quarreling
    sons, Eve's hair and Adam's hands

will ignite in sweet chaos,
    a brief fall into a world

before the Garden, before
    these rows of corn and lilies,

a time before time,
    swirling and undivided.

Carving the Hollow

Carving the Hollow

1904, the Ukraine

Grandfather leans over the violin,
wood shavings collecting
on the dirt floor. His hands,
broad and darkened with plowing,
scrape the strips of cherry wood.
He will press, bend, and glue
to create the hollow place
where the sound grows large.

Now he sits in moonlight,
tunes the strings to play
"Lonely and Defenseless,"
to let it rise out of the distance
between us.

*

1944, Kazakhstan

Inside a dirt hut his grandchildren
wait by a window heavy with ice.
A gust through the door
suddenly opened is not the mother
they are waiting for.
The child's finger through ice
makes a tunnel to see her come
at last. She will take off
her only dress and wrap it
around her naked children.

We had nothing when we escaped,
Anna tells me. No violin.

But somewhere it drifts,
and I wait to play it, to place
my cheek against its body,
the left hand curled like Grandfather
on his sickbed, while the bow
scrapes tones for a song.

*

What we call silence
is the bow lifted

while the melody persists
through the black bars

toward the final double bar,
which is only a pause.

This is the melody
in the key of O, of wonder

and sorrow. How shall I play?
This is the whole note stretching

into a bridge, the bow lifting
and falling like a hand beckoning.

I will play it again and again
so that you remember the song

and can hear it over the moaning
and the sighs. So that the hollow

of my ear can rest for awhile against
the place that is empty.

Prayer at Archangel, Siberia

This blinding light is ice,
its wing a slippery silence,
its summer thaw a broken cry.
How can a child stand upright
on a hill of shifting logs?
She balances on one piece
of bread, pulls out the quota,
her thin arms dragging one tree
after another and another,
her skirt a frozen weight
around her rag-bound feet.

> *Is mercy bound beneath*
> *this ice? The children caught*
> *in history's vise lie there.*

Angel-above-all-angels, your light
diminished in our wintry days,
guard their bones and crowns
of brittle hair, their final
stumble, and the drifting down,
arms out in frozen flight.

for Lena Wiebe, who survived

Seeing It

In memory of Daniel Wiebe, 1900-1943,
and all who died of torture in the 20th century.

1

The century opens with his small hand
which flutters—a blur that flies
and stumbles by turns. He is the one
standing alone on a station platform, waving
at the diminishing rumble while the single
eye burns its way into the night.

In the photograph, 1903, Grandfather's hands
are loose around Daniel's small hips.
I want to show you this before my own
hands become light as paper, or a cloud,
like the ones that refuse to glide over
our valley in August when the night sky
is zigzagged with shooting stars.
To write it so that you can see that Daniel
is not a blur, but wears scuffed shoes,
striped stockings, and a cap over blonde
curls, that he is wary of the photographer
who hangs black curtains on poles
in a village street, who dances behind
a box to capture Daniel's face—
moonflower beside the railroad tracks.

2

The sky showers its losses while
the world sleeps. But I stay awake
for the one meteor to fall close over
the valley where I lie on my back,
bear and dog wheeling over me,
a horse galloping over Ukrainian fields.

Imagine the black hole of everyone lost,
then holding the reins of a horse,
your own. To lie in a bed alone,
yet night after night to be shielded
by an angel with a broad back, one
that nickers at your window in the morning.
And then to become the wind, the body's
weight burning toward lightness as you ride.

Daniel leans over the steaming
newborn lamb. He washes the twitching
limbs, strips mucous from the mouth.
He learns the weight of horses,
carries a bag of remedies, lifts
the eyelids of the ones with fevers.
He will walk at last to a house
where Elizabeth waits, and will gather
his children into his lap.

1943 and Daniel is kicked toward
the open door, the bump of rails,
stench of wounds. The train scrapes
its way through the passes of the Urals.
Shouts and spitting, and he rides
the air onto sharp rocks, a clatter
of wheels fading into the fires
of his own body.

3

Fifty years later his daughter's hands
unfold a yellowed paper. It is a piece
of her father, the only one, a drawing
he made for her when she was two.
She holds it up by its corners—a lamb
filling the page, meadow flowers around
the woolly legs. She has brought it
with her from Siberia, from the orphanage
where it was her pillow.

Can you see it, the hand moving in the dark,
and hear the voice whispering behind the hand,
"She is so small," the one who rescues her?
And can you see the hand that will not move
when the trains rattle past?

Grandfather releases his long arms, and Daniel
turns his back to us. The photographer folds
the black curtain and sighs. He slides
the glass plates into a wooden box, then closes
it with a snap. You can't hear that because
a train is approaching with its single eye
and then, in a flare, is gone.

Borrowing the Horse

What you have to imagine
is my father having nothing,
and asking for everything.

She was the darling
of the village, and he
had only his good looks,

a sheaf of paper,
and three books, which he
lay down before he picked up

the reins of the borrowed
horse. This is about asking,
and about words—the way

a horse can give you an answer
by trotting in the right direction.
My father took a deep breath

and waited under that northern
sky, and the horse stood beside
with flick of skin and sideglance.

Like prayer, when all we have
is breath warming our empty hands,
and whatever the answer,
the horse is not ours to keep.

Wedding Night

August 11, 1918

In the prairie fields, wheat and wildflowers
ripen together. Even in dusk light
they swell, growing so far north.
Last light spills around the dark green shade
as she unbuttons her dress.
They have married in a hall of death.
Even then the congregation blessed them,
crowding in with coughs and damp handkerchiefs.
Im krankenheit oder gesundheit, * they promised,
and now her dark hair is tangled on the pillow
and they hold each other as though
they are already parting.
Morning will arrive with its usual fires,
like grace. Or will it be judgment,
she wonders. These hungers, this happiness—
how to hold it? "Therefore shall a man cling,"
or was it "forsake?" She must hold loosely,
take a different vow—another marriage—
as now in the darkness which arrives at last,
her husband, in deep sleep, lets her go.

In sickness or in health

49

Learning to Sing in Parts

After the quarreling at recess
my father teaches his students
to listen, to hold a pitch
and hum it, his head close

to the small child.
And the child listens and seeks
for the tone, sliding
into a float of singing,

the whole room of children
riding out now on one note.
But then, two, three,
even four tones at once,

father sorting and joining
their varied voices into
a rich and layered flow.
How to hold the note against

the other pitches? This
is the world's secret,
he confides, to enter
and be close, yet separate.

That room musty with chalk
and sweat, closed door,
and still the harmony
slips out, escaping

like most secrets do.
Alone at the end of the day,
the schoolhouse empty
and shadowed, he wonders,

can it be taught?
He seeks it too.
How patiently his own father
taught him, held him close,

his voice vibrating light and low
under the wavering melody, a duet
that hovers over the stony fields.

My Father Asks for Psalms

My father asks for Psalms his last days,
and mother reads. She skips the curses,
she tells me. Why darken his final hours?
The ark is ready, and he is safely on board
without the drowning wicked. Grace for all,
he preached, but we must choose. Human will
the victor to the last. But then, brooding,
he imagines the bloated bodies floating.
Only one ark, and drunken Noah his father?
The rain comes down, comes down, and gathers
in dark pools. The wondrous ways of God,
who can know? Will he save the lost?
"His mercy, his mercy," my mother sings
into the sheets of rain, to which he clings.

The Sailing

My mother lifts her blue-veined
    hand, "I'm ready to go."
        She stares into the white wall,

which billows into a sail.
    Little boat of bones.
        In dream she is carried

by a swift river, wearing
    a red dress. Clear water,
        and I on the bank.

But she doesn't see me.
    She has become one with motion.
        Even in water she is fire.

Child Diving

He points his small body,
arms out for the arc,

and holds his breath for the plunge,
the rise. Again and again

he breaks into the mirrored sky.
This time, in reckless joy,

he nicks his head against
the flagstone edge and rises

among the spreading stain.
I hold him then; he shivers

against my heat, I press
against his blood's release

until the doctor, with curved
needle, joins the jagged gash,

what we later love to touch
in its mending, the way we love

the ecstasy of falling, although
imperfectly into a perfect sky,

loving even its borders—
a place to fall and to be held.

Piano in the Vineyard

Night Falls on the Neighborhood

after a painting by Peter Janzen

Rows of low houses recede
into the collecting dark.
Asphalt street is iridescent

with spills of streetlamp and oil,
walkways lead to shut doors,
and palm trees scrape high

against the blackening cobalt sky.
Each house is a locked box,
separate and dimmed.

Nothing is revealed.
Only the ear pressed against
the rumble of a pillow hears

in first deep sleep the secret
of the neighborhood—that we all ride
earth's original music,

that what binds us one to the other
is ocean toss and the rise of mountains.
That God's brooding still hovers

over us, each one, each house.
And over the red car which leans against
the curb, ready to start.

Finding Words for the Moonwalk

In Norway the picture in translation
was fuzzy, and the TV spilled words
in every language, seeking the right ones
while Armstrong claimed "one giant step."
Moondust fluffed around his bobbing boots,
the wrinkled flag was planted,
and we carried our sleepy children back
to bed, pressing our lips to their foreheads.
Goodnight, was all we said in 1969
while the moon continued its circling,
its face blank and mineral.

And still the words elude us.
When I stroke the rock in the museum,
I say, "I am touching the moon,"
and feel its distance, as sometimes
when we say goodnight, lingering
before our separate journeys into the dark.
Later another astronaut in orbit
read the words "In the beginning,"
borrowing, as the moon does,
as we all do. "The beginning" we say,
yet know that words were spoken before
those words—syllables exploding
into the void. And we reach for them,
something new to steady us for our next step,
and for the spaces between.

Prophecy 2000

Anyone circling earth
at the turn of the year
would have seen how
one millennium unhinged
from another in a soft
flare of lights,
and no monster rose
to devour us,
nor did the earth split.
At the corner grocery
Mandy cracks her gum and wit,
pronouncing once again
the foolishness of humans
and tabloid headlines.
And when we enter the old
mission at winter's solstice,
we hear costumed devils curse
the prophesied birth.
No safety or success,
they shout, defying John
whose voice echoes
and rises above all warnings.
So that we strain and lean
once more toward the finale—
there, under the peeling
paint of the altar,
the promised Infant,
toward whom even the demons
creep on stone steps
to weep and sing.

Touching Millennia

These giant sequoias
in their rough coats,
their trunks like houses.

I want to touch them,
to step over the fence
and press my palms against

their skin. Last year
snowdrifts piled and I
walked close, entered

the charred cavity to lean
and stay awhile. Whole
limbs fall, large as trees,

and still they stand,
survivors of fire and saws.
"Onward for Jesus,"

the lumberers' children
sang, sitting on a jagged
stump as more trees fell.

The empty spaces still echo.
Once in moonlight I walked
in the grove and thought

I heard them breathe, long
slow breaths, like the silence
of God loosening in waves
around my small shadow.

Talking Like I Know

I say "mountain," yet have barely touched
its rocky slopes and steep inclines,
    keeping my distance.

Once I announced "brodiaea," the wildflower,
rescuing a park ranger, pure guess. And he said
    yes.

I could whisper "La Muerta," the angel who
    entered
your house, who insisted that you follow,

but the room is dark and what I hear
is "wind" and "stone," and what I lean on

is the table where I see you sitting, as before,
asking, "would I like a glass of water,"

which today sounds like "would I like to
taste the mountain," your words so heavy

with knowledge, I am afraid to say yes.

               in memory of Roberta Spear, 1948-2003

Wilderness

In all of us, the wilderness,
our nostrils flared for water,
for the crouching shadow.

We glimpse it in dreams
and in the faces of children,
their eyes glancing into

another place. In adolescents
the tender profile—Pietro's
"Young John the Baptist,"

golden curls, and under the smooth
cheek, muscles twitching.
Sometimes on a summer evening

the air presses against
our bodies with a stillness
so thin, we could break through.

Coyote call, the hawk's scream,
all of us thirsty for the unknown
as the snowmelt diminishes

into an eerie silence.
To cross over into that country
without map or tools,

to touch the source,
to kneel down and taste it.

The Words He Didn't Say

My father, his last years,
gazes at the mountain and listens.
Every morning it waits for him,
massive and glistening.
In childhood only a hill, now this.
Who can ascend the mountain,
the Psalmist asks, begging
for a pure heart. And what language
comes from purity, what voice?
Not mine beside the hospital bed,
pressing for recognition.
All those years his head turning
toward something else.
This life a preface, he would say.
The dailiness of lisp and stutter.
I want him to hear me,
to see me, to say last words.
But he can't turn around,
his path too high and narrow
in this room where now his last
breaths go out. We stand
in a silence which is immense
and open, the first vowel of a language
we have never heard before.

For My Neighbor, Dying

Flowering branches in my hand
are cut from the peach tree between us,
what unfolded when we weren't looking—
sudden pink over frozen grass.
I bring the blooms into the hospital room
where you lie under bright lights,
your hands stiff and swollen.

All these years we hurried past
this extravagance—the double-skirts,
double-scent, like a weight
until we spend it.
It isn't too late after all.
They've unlocked the dam
and the creek by your house
is running free.
Can you hear it?
Take these blossoms with you.
There are thousands more,
open and spilling into the night.

Seeking the Song

The canary flits
    from note to note
        among seed-scatter,

the small rhythms
    of her swing,
        the blurred revelations

of a pecked mirror.
    What is the path
        to the original melody,

the one which the flock
    sings as it gathers
        in those distant trees?

When Verdi paced his room,
    Violetta's voice led him
        into labyrinths where ecstasy

and loss entwine.
    Page after page,
        the writhing twists,

the search for resolution.
    Listen to the cadences
        that lead to death.

Notice what is gained,
    how in those last chords, Love,
        older than the world, gazes at you.

Piano in the Vineyard

Pruned vineyards slide past like cemeteries
in winter fog, vines bound to wires.

One vineyard after another. And I remember
the white markers of childhood, of fatal crashes,

five clustered crosses for my friends,
how I found solace at the piano, hammered

the keys, my fingers pressing into the massive
weight. Row after row, the contorted vines,

the furrows empty now of laborers who bent
aching in the cold, then stumbled into drafty

shacks for sleep. Wounds of the living.
The child awake at night, branches scratching

the window, chimney's howl, and the morning clang
of the stove's cold mouth. The woman awake

at night, remembering, her arms extended,
her fingers tracing the echoing cadences.

*

Repeat, repeat, the scales ascending and descending,
octaves and arpeggios which lead into the shimmers

of Ravel, patterns and shifting chords, not
for themselves but for the vast stretches.

The measures over and over, like waves lifting
and falling back into the deep, burning cold,

what I glimpsed when a child, and then a bride.
When the wrecking ball shattered the apartment wall,

there stood a piano, upright against wallpaper roses,
abandoned. Three floors up the narrow stairs

and it was mine, this giant wooden heart with its
demands, and large enough for me to enter.

*

Black vines of Majorca, and in the distance
a sheen of surf. February sun, bud and stem

still hidden. During the storms of 1839,
his beloved piano still floating at sea,

Chopin sits, a cup of hot tea in his stained
hands as the children clamor about in the small,

smoky rooms. He marks the pages, slashing,
presses the borrowed keys, inking more notes

until he finds the harmonic shift and pace
which will ignite the coal. Rain, incessant

rain, one prelude after another, separate and touching
until each blazes up whole in its beauty and sorrow,

and his piano finally touches shore.

*

Pianos everywhere—in living rooms, schools,
bars, tuned and untuned, the strings resounding.

That broken one leaning against the edge
of the vineyard, the one on which our children

played Chopsticks, and a chicken flew out.
Rows of faces leaning into the keyboard,

hands spread, the whole body bending.
"How do you get to Carnegie Hall? Practice,

practice." Rubenstein at eighty walking on stage,
stiff and small. He creaks onto the bench

and plays a stream, and then a torrent,
his hands like water.

*

On Holy Saturday my husband finds a dead vine
in our garden, mounts it on a cross of grapestakes.

The branches have hands, fingers spread, the head
a rounded joint, the torso a twist of life

gone out. *Lose your life to find it.*
This is the end of striving, but not of music,

only a pause before the next movement,
which is the first and last fire. Every harvest

is rehearsal—heft of swollen grapes cut,
branch springing back, leaves flaming

over and over before our last breath.
To live in the rhythm of such outpouring, releasing

ourselves. Life and death as light as that,
wheeling between earth and heaven, then spilling over.

In Umbria

Blackbird sings all night,
    pours his silken notes
        into the hollows of our sleep.

Fireflies float into our room,
    bright globes gliding.
        They do not doubt their glow

or origin, drift easily out
    the window and over the canyon.
        And all around, the hills

are etched in silver,
    their winding roads like ribbons,
        loose and lifting.

The whole world is lit
    from within, this soft darkness
        only a veneer, here

where our hands seek
    the other, and grow light as wings
        through the burning leaves.

November Night

Tonight the ash tree
is a Byzantine dome
dropping its gold
piece by piece

as the sky lowers
its ripe stars.
Never has a night
been so clear.

Immensity of dome
over dome, closer
now, touching
my head.

After the green commotion
of summer, this stillness.
Not the intimacy
of death, but of presence,

that tiny hollow
on the twig, the place
of clinging growing large
as it fills.

Falling Asleep
Under the Full-Blown Rose

These are the nights
before last loosening,

late delights
among the pollens

before the stem stands upright
and uncrowned.

My heart rehearses losing
by skipping beats;

thinning arteries bruise
my breasts and arms

as light refuses
the rosy folds,

and I drift, slack
and softened,

down into the dark—
scent of rootcellar,

the seeds of stars.

Between the Layers

"Every true poem is a spark,
and aspires to the condition of the original fire,
arising out of the emptiness." Charles Wright

Old wounds, these words,
     layered under bare limbs—

shattered crowns of peach trees,
     the vineyard's crimson scrawl

lying now in molding carpets
     of slow burn, words that wait

in cold mud. Not a scarred
     healing, but to become new

with a quick flare.
     Not the long darkness

of disintegration, and yet,
     out of that abyss, the spark.

Pascal sewed it into the layers
     of his coat: "Since about half-past

ten, until about half-past midnight,
     fire, certitude, feeling, peace, joy."

That fire.

About the Author

Jean Wiebe Janzen was born in Saskatchewan, was raised in the midwestern United States, and now lives in Fresno, California.

She completed her undergraduate studies at Fresno Pacific University and received the Master of Arts at California State University of Fresno. Her previous books are *Words for the Silence* (1984), *Three Mennonite Poets* (1986), *The Upside-Down Tree* (1992), *Snake in the Parsonage* (1995), and *Tasting the Dust* (2000).

She was selected for The Creative Writing Fellowship from the National Endowment for the Arts for her poetry.

Janzen's poetry has been published in *Poetry, Gettysburg Review, Prairie Schooner, Image, Christian Century, Poetry International, The Common Reader, The Great River Review,* and *Cincinnati Poetry Review.*

Among the poetry collections in which her poems appear are *A Cappella: Mennonite Voices in Poetry* (University of Iowa Press), *Highway 99: A Literary Journey Through California's Great Central Valley* (Heyday Books), and *What Will Suffice: Contemporary American Poets on the Art of Poetry* (Peregrine Smith Books).